WHITSTABLE and ʹAR

Books by the same author:

Thomas Clark of Canterbury (1775–1859)
The Seasalter Company — a Smuggling Fraternity (1740–1854)
Seasalter and the Mystery of Robinson Crusoe

First Printed	*October 1971*
Second Impression	*January 1978*
Third Impression	*November 1983*
Fourth Impression	*June 1985*
Fifth Impression	*June 1988*

© **WALLACE HARVEY**

ISBN 0 9508564 2 8

Text set in Baskerville 11pt

*Printed and Published in Great Britain by
Emprint Publications, 9 Harbour Street, Whitstable, Kent CT5 1AG*

Acknowledgments

While much of the information has been gathered from the old files of the Kentish Gazette and sources too numerous to record, yet I must acknowledge the invaluable assistance I have received from Janet Binns, Philip Jakeman, Frank Newsome, Donald Rodgers, Kingsley Empett and Barry Johnstone, all of whom have in some measure made this publication possible.

Wallace Harvey

Whitstable
and the
French Pris

oners of War

by
Wallace
Harvey

List of Illustrations   Page

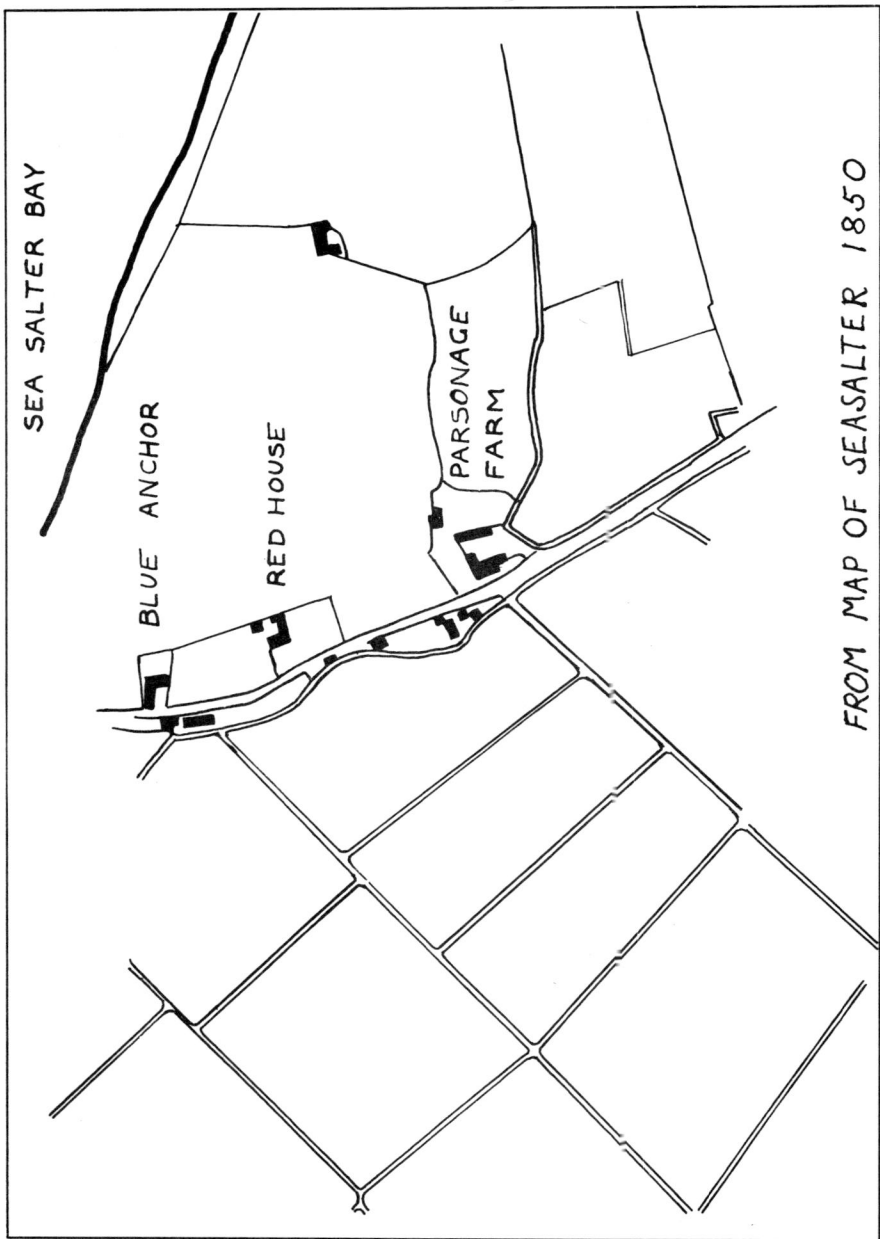

SEA SALTER BAY

BLUE ANCHOR

RED HOUSE

PARSONAGE FARM

FROM MAP OF SEASALTER 1850

..... the prisoners

A lucrative and successful variation of the smuggling activities at Whitstable was the assistance given to the escaping prisoners of war between the years 1793 and 1814.

During that comparatively short period of twenty one years vast numbers of prisoners of war were brought to England, and they consequently filled to over-flowing all the available places of confinement. Great prison camps were established at places like Dartmoor and Norman Cross. Many prisoners were also billeted in Parole Towns. But by far the worst fate befel those many who were confined in the living hell of the Prison Ships. These were hulks which were moored in various harbours round the coast such as Portsmouth, Langston or Gosport, but principally in the rivers such as the Thames and Medway.

At one time there were upwards of sixty such hulks filled to overflowing, a damning testimony of man's inhumanity to man. Those stationed along the Thames from Woolwich to Sheerness provided a constant source of supply of desperate men who were so hopeless that, despite their manacles and leg chains, they were willing to face death by drowning or by suffocation in the oozy mud of the river banks, or by being shot on sight. Anyone familiar with the dreary Saltings along the lower reaches of the Thames or the mouth of the Medway will appreciate the awful natural conditions which those poor half-starved creatures had to face in their bid for freedom. For the great majority death was the only merciful release from their terrible sufferings. It was reported without compunction that almost one in three died each year, and it was obvious that few people knew or cared what was happening.

The Transport Office which had the care of the prisoners was notorious for its slackness and corruption. Even a casual knowledge of history is sufficient to reveal that the Government was rotten with jobbery, bribery and double dealing. After Captain Charles Dupin had regained his liberty, he wrote a report for the French Government.

"The Medway," he reported, "is covered with men-of-war, dismantled and lying in ordinary. It is in these floating tombs that prisoners of war are buried alive. They are lodged on the lower deck, on the upper deck and even on the orlop deck. Four hundred malefactors are the maximum of such a ship appropriated to convicts. From eight hundred to twelve hundred is the ordinary number of prisoners of war heaped together in a prison ship of the same rate". What with the very casual attitude of those in authority to their responsibility to the embarrassing number of prisoners, the appallingly high death rate, and the readiness of the poorly paid guards to accept bribes, it was not altogether difficult to maintain a constant stream of escapers, or indeed to conceal the escapes for some time. A favourite and common mode of escape was to jump into the water as if committing suicide then to hang on to the anchor chains under the water with only the nose above water concealed by a massive link. If the act was observed the sentry might even fire his musket, but the swiftly flowing current together with the cumbersome chains would give the impression of a quick death, a frequent occurrence. Then when the excitement had died down the prisoner endeavoured to drop down with the current to a place from which he could be picked up by a passing boat. The second mode was to quietly slip away from a labouring gang and trust to the desolate Saltings for security.

. . . . . plan of escape

Both of these methods offered but a slim chance of success unless assistance was at hand. Fortunately, however, many of the escapes were organised and timed by the Whitstable smugglers. Yawls and cutters from Whitstable sailed regularly every week across the Channel to Flushing, Dunkirk or Ostend and consequently provided a ready means of transport for the escapers which did not arouse too much suspicion.

The first objective was to contact the relatives of the prisoner and arrange for sufficient money for ransom or bribery. This having been satisfactorily arranged it was only a matter of time before the prisoner was located in whichever camp, hulk, prison or town in which he was detained and instructions given him on how and when to make his bid for freedom. If he was poor he was expected to make his own way to London and so on to the Whitstable boats. If however, the ransom money was sufficient or he was an important person, he would be collected by a specially built wagon or two horse chaise and transported either to London, or if Whitstable was too closely watched, to one of the other Kent sea ports.

It was usual for the chaise to travel through the daytime, stop at a small wood on the outskirts of a town to unload the prisoners at dusk, and then go on to friendly inns in the town for supplies and to stable the horses. At daybreak the chaise would resume its innocent looking journey and pick up the prisoners along the road on the far side of the town.

On reaching London the Frenchmen, singly or in pairs, made their way to the Custom House Quay, the Wool Quay, Beals Wharf, Tooley Street, or Chester and Brewers Quay. Here they would be sure to find one of the Whitstable fleet of Hoys ready to take them on the next stage of their journey. Hoys were vessels so named because they were engaged in the coasting trade! For centuries they maintained a regular and rapid means of transport between Whitstable and London by taking advantage of the current of the river and the fast flowing tides. At the period in question a fleet of twenty such vessels was engaged in this very useful and indeed necessary trade.

In addition to the Hoys, were the two Oyster Market boats which sailed up to Billingsgate every day, and also quite a number of private fishing yawls which took their own catch.

Some two miles to the west of Whitstable Harbour, close to

1

the sea shore at Seasalter, stands the Blue Anchor public house,[2] the successor of a far more ancient inn. The sea at this point ebbs some two miles from the shore exposing acres of firm sand flats. For hundreds of years the tenants of the Dean and Chapter of Canterbury cultivated oysters, gathered cockles, and maintained fish weirs on these wide sand flats. Far out on the tide line near to the point of the Pollard Sand stood a high timber platform where the market boats could moor and load at all states of the tide and where the fisher folk took and cleaned their daily catch. At the same time there was stranded about four hundred yards off the shore at the Blue Anchor the hulk of an old brig on which the oyster people lived when they were working there. Moreover during the season quite a number of wild fowlers used hides like half barrels sunk in the mud, or punts over the shallow water. In consequence of these numerous legitimate activities within the area it is easy to realise that there would be many ready and willing to give cover and assistance to the French escapers. During the hours of daylight the prisoners could

2

land on the high platform if the tide was in, or wade ashore if the tide was out, mix with the people working there to avoid detection and then continue their bid for freedom when darkness fell. During the hours of darkness it was far easier to pass as a wildfowler or someone returning from the fish weirs after attending to them at low tide. Having landed the prisoners the vessel was then able to proceed to its moorings at the Horsebridge at Whitstable and survive any examination by the Customs.

Once one of the Hoys was unable to unload its human cargo at the usual place because the whole gang were chained together. The vessel consequently sailed straight on past Whitstable to the eastward to where a long shingle bank called the Street projects upwards of half a mile to sea at right angles to the shore. Here they were lanced to make their way ashore as best they could under cover of darkness. As a sequel, when Shepherds Cot, which stood in Castle Road, almost opposite the junction with Queens Road, was pulled down about forty years ago, upwards of two hundredweight of rusty iron manacles were found underneath the floor.

To the west of the Blue Anchor the desolate coastal marshes, intersected by many dykes, stretch for miles. Today they are familiar to thousands as the site of large caravan camps. At the time of the Napoleonic Wars however the area was very isolated, and many a reed grown dyke provided welcome shelter for the prisoners until it was safe for them to proceed on the next stage of their journey. Their next objective was to reach Pye Alley Farm,[14] which lies at the bottom of Clapham Hill on the main Whitstable to Canterbury Turnpike Road, about two miles S.E. of Seasalter. This farm had for some years been in the occupation of Mr. Joseph Daniels, but he having died on Saturday August 11th 1787 aged 47 years, the farm was taken over by his son-in-law, Mr. Thomas Goodwin who was an important member of the gang which organised the escapes. He found this activity so profitable that on October 19th 1797 he was able to buy out his two sisters-in-law, and thereby become the sole owner. The objective was to get the prisoners to Pye Alley Farm from their hiding places in the marshes and supply them with the very necessary clothes and food before passing them on to fresh places of concealment. Goodwin always kept at the least four fast riding horses ready for instant use. When the escaped prisoners were on the move he informed the town by riding at a gallop down and up the main street. Thus alerted the local people were ever ready to give what assistance was needed, act as watchers for approaching danger, or supply clothing or food for the starving men. When the preparations had been made, Mr. Goodwin would idly ride his horse along the route to be followed by the prisoners, pausing at intervals as if viewing the countryside in order to allow them to see him from their places of concealment. They would then follow at a safe distance ready to dive for cover should the need arise.

The route followed from the seashore was the present road leading from the Blue Anchor to Seasalter Cross. Then on up

the narrow Church Lane with its high protective banks to where it is now crossed by the Thanet Way. Since the first World War houses and caravan camps have sprung up along this length of road and made it much frequented, but before that time it was quite isolated. Until recent years the next section of the route rejoiced in the expressive name of Cut Throat Lane,[10] but in these more sensitive times it has become Pilgrims Lane. This delightful relic of a more rural age, with its high bank and obscuring hedges, rapidly ascends to the hills and commands unsurpassed views over miles of flat marshes[11] and up the Swale to the westward. At its highest point it joins Foxes Cross,[12] a junction of four lanes. To the left is a lane ascending to yet higher ground of Wraik Hill. On the right the road descends the very steep Foxes Hill to Foxes Bottom, Yorkletts, and the marshes. Straight in front stretches the old road to Pean Hill and Canterbury. For centuries it was known as Seasalter Lane but it has recently been renamed Foxes Cross Road. Despite the greedily destroying hand of civilization the area surrounding these lanes remains a delightfully unspoilt tract of Old England.

11

12

Proceeding some hundred yards along Foxes Cross Road a small lane branches to the left and takes on the name of Pye Alley Lane[13] It is an unspoilt length of rural road which follows the foot of the hilly country which rises to the north while towards the south, after some open country, stretch the many acres of Ellenden Woods, part of the Forest of Blean.

After following the lone horseman along this secluded lane for some distance the prisoners would be drawing near to Pye Alley Farm[14] a most important link in their escape route. If

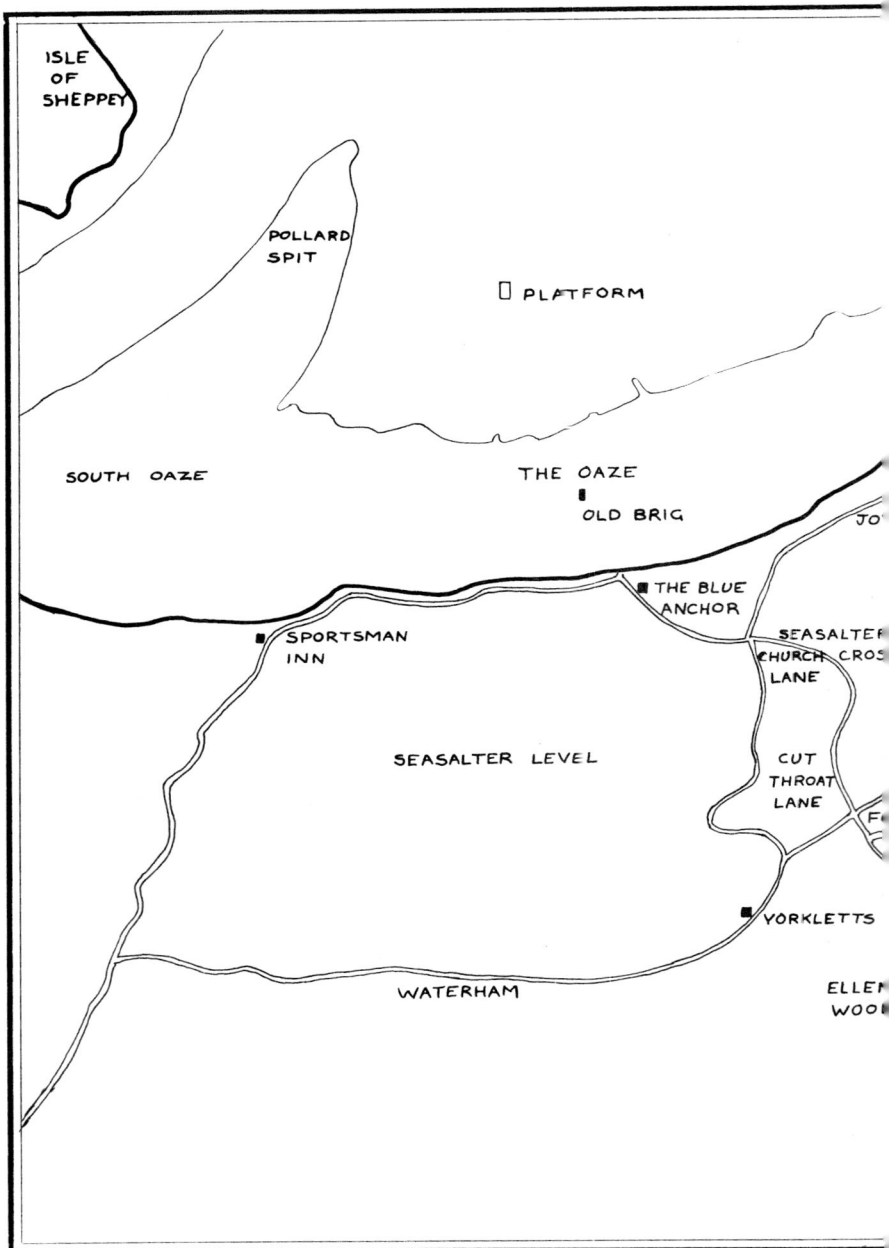

ISLE
OF
SHEPPEY

POLLARD
SPIT

☐ PLATFORM

SOUTH OAZE

THE OAZE
■
OLD BRIG

JO

■ THE BLUE
ANCHOR

■ SPORTSMAN
INN

SEASALTER
CHURCH CROS
LANE

SEASALTER LEVEL

CUT
THROAT
LANE

F

■ YORKLETTS

WATERHAM

ELLEN
WOO

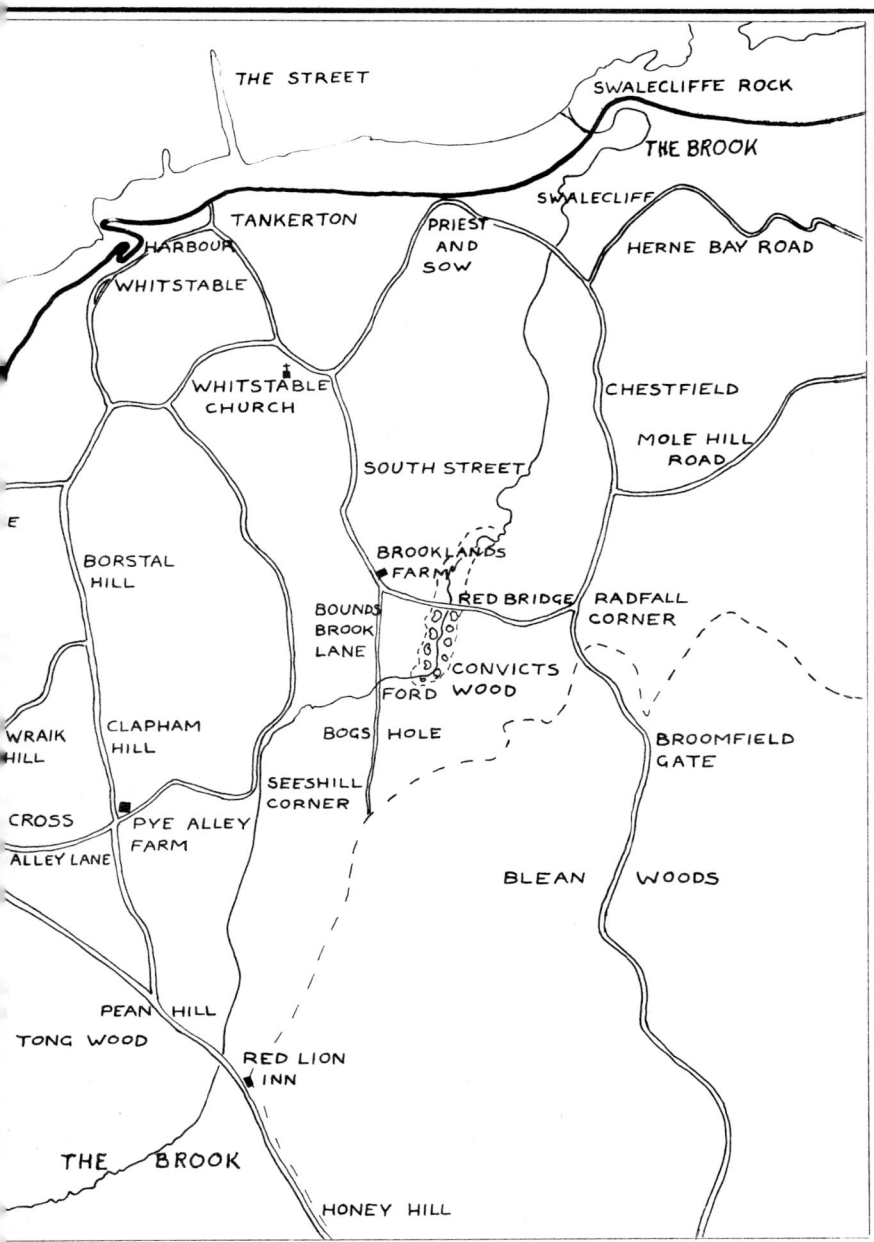

THE STREET

SWALECLIFFE ROCK

THE BROOK

SWALECLIFF

TANKERTON

PRIEST
AND
SOW

HERNE BAY ROAD

HARBOUR

WHITSTABLE

WHITSTABLE
CHURCH

CHESTFIELD

MOLE HILL
ROAD

SOUTH STREET

E

BORSTAL
HILL

BROOKLANDS
FARM

RED BRIDGE

RADFALL
CORNER

BOUNDS
BROOK
LANE

CONVICTS
FORD WOOD

WRAIK
HILL

CLAPHAM
HILL

BOGS HOLE

BROOMFIELD
GATE

SEESHILL
CORNER

CROSS

ALLEY LANE

PYE ALLEY
FARM

BLEAN WOODS

PEAN HILL

TONG WOOD

RED LION
INN

THE BROOK

HONEY HILL

they saw a light shining from the house they knew that it was safe to approach. The light shone from a tir y window about ten inches square, hard up under the eaves over the side door.[16] This little window, still there at the present day, only allowed the light to be seen by those approaching from Seasalter or Canterbury.[15] The more wealthy or fortunate prisoners were brought from Canterbury on horses or in chaises supplied by the landlord of the Fountain. Having been fitted out with

any necessary clothes and food, the prisoners continued to follow the twisting little Bogs Hole Lane to the eastward for half a mile until, at Seeshill Corner, they met the Bogs Hole Brook.[18]Here they were left to their own devices to follow the

18

28

thickly wooded banks of the brook as it meandered through
the meadows towards the sea. After following the brook for a
distance they arrived at a point where the copse widened out
to form a woodland which rejoiced in the significant name of
Convicts Wood. For some this secluded wood was to be their
home for perhaps months, until darkness, tide and safety,
made it possible to attempt the next desperate part of their
journey. Meanwhile the little stream provided an ample
supply of fresh drinking and washing water and the farmer at
Bounds Brook Farm, now Brooklands Farm,[20] supplied them
with food. During their enforced period of hiding the
Frenchmen often occupied themselves in making small
workboxes, decorated outside with coloured paper and split
oat straw, with which they expressed their gratitude to the
kindly people who cared for them. One of these boxes has
survived to the present day.[22] At the appropriate time they

were given the signal to follow the course of the stream through Chestfield to Swalecliffe, to an old inn which stood quite near to the brook where the Herne Bay Road now crosses it, called the Old Fan.[23]Here in the barn they were given food for their voyage and then conducted the short distance to the sea shore where the brook enters the sea[26]on the west side of Swalecliffe Rock[25]The Rock was a high bank of shingle and land projecting a considerable distance into the sea, but which during the last fifty years has suffered severe erosion.

Screened by the dark shadow of this high bank the escapers were able either to walk unseen to a waiting ship or to row out to it according to the state of the tide. Naturally the chances against their detection were strengthened by a dark moonless night or a sea mist. By day break the next morning they were, with very few exceptions, safely deposited on the other side of the Channel.

As the escape route was never discovered, and the smugglers rarely caught, very little factual information has been recorded. Brief insights into the subject may be had from the reports of the few court cases of those brought to justice. Fortunately, fifty years ago there were many still living who had heard from their grandparents all about this interesting variation of smuggling. Those who took an active part in the events were well-known and respected for their veracity. Although it is fairly easy to estimate the number of vessels and persons engaged in transporting the prisoners from London and the banks of the Thames, it is far more difficult to say how many took them over the Channel because most of the local smugglers regularly took prisoners and guineas to the Continent and returned with contraband.

. . . . . the infamous James Moore

The most famous escape agent, although so well known in Whitstable, was nevertheless a great mystery, a veritable Scarlet Pimpernel. He appeared on the scene as a dashing

young man with plenty of money, highly educated, able to speak French as fluently as English, yet such an accomplished liar that it was doubtful if he himself knew when he was telling the truth. Later in life he claimed to have been born at Fordwich near Canterbury on August 12th 1788, and he then went under the name of James Moore. It is most certain that the family of Moore had been resident there for several generations. At the same time he claimed to have been apprenticed at the age of fourteen in the year 1802 to Mr. Mantell, Shipwright and Boat-builder of Deal. This is most curious because although it has not been possible to identify a boatbuilder of that name at Deal, the family of Mantell had been domiciled in Fordwich for as long as that of Moore, and in such a small place the two families must have been well acquainted with each others history. Moreover there is ample evidence that Sir Thomas Mantell, who was Mayor of Dover six times from 1795 onwards, found in Moore a perpetual embarrassment. Sir Thomas was well acquainted with Fordwich as his grandfather was Rector there. He had been educated to be a surgeon but gave up that profession to be the Government Agent for the exchange of Prisoners of War at Dover, and after the Peace of 1815 he became Agent for the Mail Packets. It will thus be seen how the subsequent activities of Moore must have been a constant source of annoyance to him. If indeed Moore did complete an apprenticeship anywhere he would most probably have been about twenty one when he arrived in Whitstable and promptly bought the well-known hoy called the Whitstable. She had been built at Whitstable in 1778, her official number was 9756; she was classed as a Smack of 13 tons and her measurements were 30'0 x 10'5" x 5'3". Until 1785 she was owned by Daniel Howard and James Nicholson, then until May 1st 1787, when that partnership was dissolved, by David Howard and Thomas Reynolds. Howard was reputed to have been quite successful as a smuggler, but things did not go well for him and he hung himself in the Isle of Sheppey in April 1792. It will be seen from this that the vessel was far from new when she was purchased by Moore and used to transport the escaped prisoners from London to Seasalter. The business undoubtedly proved successful, for Moore bought a second boat called the Two Sisters with which he accomplished the final stage of the escape to the Continent. Apparently his activities were well-known to those in authority but no serious efforts seem to have been made to apprehend him. The Two Sisters was quite a large vessel of her type, classed as of 35 tons, and her regular and reliable cross channel runs were often used by those in the highest authority for their own secret ends. Probably in connection with his espionage Moore now began to use various other names such as James Feaste Moore or Thomas Feaste Moore. In the ports of East Kent he was known by the name of Captain Thomas Harman, a name which he took from a well-known Whitstable family. It is indeed truly difficult to find an adequate explanation for his amazing success, his many influential friends in high places on both sides of the Channel and his ability to organise escapes from any part of the kingdom.

On March 22nd and 23rd 1810 he tried to organise the escape of two very important prisoners, and officialdom was compelled at last to take some action. These people were none other than General Pillet, Adjutant Commandant Chef de l'Etat — Major of the First Division of the Army of Portugal and Commander Paolucci of the Friedland. They were met half a mile from their quarters at Alresford by Captain Thomas Harman in a post-chaise in which they were driven to Winchester. Alighting in a back street they kept out of sight while Harman went to get fresh horses and another chaise. From Winchester they drove by round-about ways through Croydon, Sevencaks, Tunbridge, Robertsbridge and Battle, to Hastings. Apparently Harman thought it was too dangerous to bring them to Whitstable, and told them that he took this route as it was necessary for safety. In any case it would have been very difficult for such exalted persons to travel with the common herd then passing through Whitstable. Harman told his charges not to worry and he would get them safely across in thirty-four hours as he had General Osten.

They arrived at Hastings at 7.0 p.m. on March 23rd and alighted outside the town while Harman went on to arrange for their lodgings. After a while he returned and conducted them to the house of Mrs. Akers, a one eyed woman. This is most interesting as there were families of that name living at Whitstable where the postman was James Akers, and one could almost surmise some connection. However, the prisoners remained concealed at her house for four days while they waited for favourable weather. It was known that the Government agents must have had strong suspicions as to where their quarry was hidden, so for greater security they were smuggled into the house of one named Paine. The Agents were hot on their trail and even searched the house, but the room where they were concealed was kept locked and described as an empty lumber room. After two days General Pillet became thoroughly disgusted at the delay and that evening threatened to go to the Mayor and give himself up. Mr. Paine, in desperation, brought them some sailors clothes and said that two women were waiting to take them where they pleased. The prisoners proudly refused to put on such common clothes, went out, and were met by Elizabeth Akers and Rachel Hutchinson. This was the moment the watchers had been waiting for and, instead of being taken to the Mayor, the General was surrounded and arrested. Throughout the past six days, Thomas Harman had been discreetly out of sight at a well-known smugglers' inn some three miles out of town at Hollington Corner. However, the authorities knew where he was and he was soon arrested. During the examination which followed Harman swore that he did not know them to be escaped prisoners, but thought they were Guernsey lace merchants.

General Pillet and Commander Paolucci were promptly sent off to Norman Cross, and Captain Harman was put in Horsham jail. At the next examination evidence was given that Harman had bought a boat for the escape from a man who understood that it was to be used for smuggling purposes by two Guernsey lace men. The Mayor of Hastings gave it as his opinion that no Hastings petty jury would commit Harman for trial, though a grand jury might. As it was, the jury decided to take their courage in their hands and proceed with the trial. While in Horsham jail Harman was interviewed by several important people including Jones the

Solicitor to the Admiralty. He showed the Solicitor an iron crown which he said had been given him by the French Government, but which was proved to have been stolen from Paolucci's trunk. Finding that his influential friends were unable to obtain his release, Harman made a bid for himself by offering to make important disclosures to the Government regarding the escape business, and its connection with the smugglers. Much to his disgust, his offer was declined and he was sent to serve in the Navy. "He could not have been disposed of in a way less expected or more objectionable to himself", wrote the Admiralty Solicitor to Alexander McLeay the Secretary of the Transport Office, Dorset Square, Westminster. After serving for a short time on the Enterprise, Harman was sent to the Namur, the guardship at the Nore. This was much more to his liking for he was soon able to put into operation the escape procedure which he had so well organised for others. Almost before those in charge knew he was on the Namur, he was back again safely at Whitstable. In fact his escape was not recognised officially for another two years.

Meanwhile, back at Whitstable he found that the escape route had been working quite smoothly in his enforced absence, and that there was plenty of money waiting for him. He now appears to have dropped the name of Thomas Harman and adopted the name of Thomas Feaste Moore. His next exploit revealed yet another bewildering change of name, for he decided to get married to a Whitstable girl. The entry in the Marriage Register at All Saints Church gives the following information.

June 18th 1811 Theodore Eugene Feaste of the Island of Guernsey and Mary Ann Andrews of this Parish by licence.

Mary was the daughter of Thomas Andrews the landlord of the Hoy Public House. They were married by Charles Eaton Plater, Vicar of Seasalter and curate of Whitstable. From this it would appear that Feaste was still only twenty two when he married.

In order to cater for the prosperous cross Channel trade he then bought a Whitstable smack called the Elizabeth. She was a comparatively new vessel having been built at Sittingbourne

in 1803, a yawl of 16 tons, 29′3″ x 11′1″ x 5′2″. During
the next few weeks after his marriage Feaste seemed to be as
elusive and restless as ever. He made several trips to London
on his hoy the Whitstable, and also down to Broadstairs. He
was back at Whitstable again on July 4th when the Whitstable
arrived with an important prisoner from Tiverton who had
broken his parole. So important a man could not be expected
to mix with the common classes in Convicts Wood, and he
was consequently given lodgings in the Hoy Public House
where Feaste had his headquarters. Here he was able to meet
with Feaste who had only been introduced to him as the man
who could further his escape. The Frenchman could evidently romance almost as well as his agile minded acquain-
tance, for he described himself as a Jerseyman who had a
licence to take his boat to France, and of course Feaste saw
in him good game and promised to help him. Evidently
Feaste must have put on a great air of simplicity or gullibility
for the Frenchman described how his vessel had been seized
by the Customs as she had some English goods in her, and he
very much wanted to get to France. Feaste craftily promised
to help but did not reveal anything to lead him to suppose
that he knew him to be an escaped prisoner. Those who still
remember the dingey old bar of the Hoy will appreciate how
appropriate a setting it was for the shady conduct of the
skilful escape agent. With a glib tongue he described the
fearful dangers the Frenchman would have to face, warned
him that he would most certainly be stopped and searched,
and not only persuaded him to pay ten guineas for taking
him round the coast to Deal, which was all he would promise
to do, he also persuaded him to confide his watch and £18 to
his care. Then, having seen the Frenchman safely on board
the Elizabeth, Feaste decided to make himself scarce. He
made a round trip in his vessel the Two Sisters. First to
Broadstairs, then over to France, and finally back again to
Dover where the Two Sisters was found untenanted with her
name painted out. Feaste had been landed by Lieutenant
Peace of the armed cutter Decoy. He had actually persuaded
Peace that he bore important dispatches from France to John
Wilson Croker the first Secretary at the Admiralty, Charing
Cross. The Lieutenant not only brought him ashore but took

him to the Coaching Inn where he got a fast Mail Coach for London. Feaste, as crafty as ever, made some excuse to leave the coach at Canterbury and was soon back again in Whitstable, but feeling that things were getting too hot for him, he lost no time in getting away to the west of England. In the meantime the Elizabeth had sailed with the Frenchman on board. Just as Feaste had forecast she was captured while lying in Broadstairs Roads by the Lion cutter on August 24th. When he was examined the Frenchman confessed that he had broken his parole at Tiverton but refused to disclose his real name, and persisted in calling himself Nicholas Trelawney. By this time Feaste was very busy in the west country, working under the name of Thomas Herbert. He lived at Mr. Parnells, the White Lion, St. Sidwells and, apparently having plenty of money, he bought yet another boat from Mr. Owen of Topsham. Thus prepared he went off to Crediton and arranged with four prisoners to escape, helped them safely on board and did not leave them until they were safely over the Bar at Exmouth.

The capture of the Elizabeth at Broadstairs compelled Officialdom at last to recognise the fact that James Moore, alias Captain Thomas Harman, alias Thomas Feaste Moore, alias Thomas Maitland, alias Thomas Herbert, alias Theodore Eugene Feaste, had indeed escaped from the Namur and was active in his old calling.

He was such a powerful, elusive character, with so many friends in high places, having the advantage of a highly skilled organisation, that the only effective method to deal with him was to trap him through the agency of one who was conversant with his activities.

The Government could find no one better for this purpose than Sir Thomas Mantell, the Mayor of Dover and the Agent of the Transport Board for the Exchange of Prisoners, who had apparently known Moore all his life, and by virtue of his office could be well calculated to know much about his activities. Mantell was therefore instructed to get on his track and if possible apprehend him.

The report that Mantell made left no shadow of doubt that

there was not much about Feaste which he did not know. He described his usual mode of procedure, how the French prisoners having been duly approached, the terms agreed upon, the horses, chaises, boats with sails, oars, charts and provisions arranged for, he would meet them at a little distance outside their place of confinement after dark, travel all night, and with good luck get them off within two days at the outside. He said that Feaste was always flush with money and that his usual charge for his services was £100 for every four prisoners. Evidently Mantell did not know of the regular escape route through Whitstable, but was well aware of the assistance given to more wealthy prisoners which of course hurt him most. Feaste, he said, was well known to be able to speak French fluently, but he never used that language in the presence of Englishmen, he was most thorough in all his plans and business arrangements. He kept a complete account of all the depots and parole places in England, with the ranks of all the principal prisoners. As a rule he made sure of getting letters of recommendation from all the officers whose escapes he safely negotiated, and he enjoyed the confidence of some of the principal prisoners in England and Scotland. Mantell appears to have picked up the trail when the Two Sisters was found at Dover with her name painted out, but despite all his knowledge, all his diligent research, he always seemed to be several steps behind his quarry. Throughout October and November 1811 he stuck manfully to his task of trying to catch up with the man who had been a constant source of annoyance to him for so many years.

The Kentish Gazette of December 31st 1811 reveals how Mantell finally achieved his object. It appears that about the 14th December Feaste had sailed from Herne Bay with a crew of five mariners belonging to Hearn. Previous to that he had spent some weeks at Whitstable. On Friday December 27th he left Dunkirk with a cargo of silks and contraband spirits and in the afternoon of that day was captured at the back of the Goodwin Sands. His vessel was taken into Dover Harbour, where, turning on all his old charm, he was permitted to come ashore, and then in consequence of his showing important letters addressed to several Ministers of State, and also stating that he was employed by the

Admiralty to obtain information of the state of the enemy's preparations, he was given every consideration. By the time however that the news of his arrival had got through to Mantell on the Saturday morning it was too late, Feaste had left the City of London Inn at six-thirty the previous evening by the Mail Coach for London. Arriving in Canterbury at 9.0 p.m. he decided, quite unnecessarily, and certainly foolishly, to break his journey. Perhaps a fleeting visit to Whitstable under cover of darkness was uppermost in his mind. However, he arrived back at the Coach Office just before nine o'clock on the Sunday evening and was just about to take his place on the coach when he was recognised by John Abbot who was a brewer of St. Dunstans Street, Canterbury and also a County Magistrate. Abbot had just received a secret message from Mantell asking him to keep his eyes open for the much wanted man. Feaste on his part, sensing the danger he was in, quickly gave the coachman the instruction to call for him at the Kings Arms Public House in St. Peters Street. He arrived there safely and ordered a drink, but was apprehended before he had the chance to drink it.

He was taken into custody under the name of James Feaste and charged with being concerned in aiding and assisting French prisoners and other foreigners to escape from the country. Information was given that the attention of the Government had for some months past been directed to his apprehension, and warrants were issued by the magistrates for that purpose. Intimation of what had happened was sent to Mantell and the prisoner was committed by the Mayor for further examination. When the examination was resumed on the Monday the prisoner admitted that he had already been convicted on a similar charge, that he had occasionally carried over a French prisoner for the purpose of obtaining the favour of the French Government, and more readily procuring the information required. What seemed to worry the authorities far more was what had happened the previous August when he had relieved a most important Frenchman of his watch and £18. He could little have realised how very important that Frenchman was, the power he had, and the embarrassment that his recapture would cause to the English

Government, even if the country was at war with France. In order to conceal the real reason Feaste was charged comprehensively with, "Robbing the prisoners of their property whenever they were in his power and the opportunity offered itself". The Mayor soon realised that he had something far too hot to hold, and it was also said that he was deeply involved in the business himself. He therefore decided not to give Feaste up to Mantell but to send him straight up to London to Bow Street. The prisoner was accordingly sent off in grand style under a proper guard in a post-coach with four horses.

With Feaste in their hands the Authorities endeavoured to explore the whole system of aided escapes and authorised one, Charles Jones, an Admiralty solicitor, to draw up a report detailing therein the various methods by which the escapes of paroled French prisoners were effected. "They are of two kinds" he said.

1. By means of smugglers and those connected with them on the coast, who proceed with horses and covered carriages to depots and by arrangement rendezvous about the hour of the evening when the prisoners ought to be within doors, about the mile limit, and thus carry them off, travelling through the night and in the daytime hiding in woods and coverts. The horses they use are excellent and the carriages constructed for the purpose. The prisoners are conveyed to the coast, where they are delivered over to the smugglers, and concealed until the boat is ready. They embark at night and before morning are in France. These escapes are generally in pursuance of orders received from France.

2. By means of persons of prolifiquate lives who, residing in or near the Parole Towns, act as conductors to such of the prisoners as choose to form their own plan of escape. These prisoners generally travel in post-chaises, and the conductors business is to pay the expenses and give orders on the road to the innkeepers, drivers etc., to prevent discovery or suspicion as to the quality of the travellers. When once a prisoner reaches a public house or inn near the coast, he is considered safe. But there are cases when

the prisoners having one among themselves who can speak good English, travel without conductors. In these cases the innkeepers and post-boys alone are to blame, and it is certain that if this description of persons could be compelled to do their duty many escapes would be prevented. The landlord of the Fountain at Canterbury has been known to furnish chaises towards the coast for six French prisoners at a time without a conductor. As a rule the prisoners made their way to London, from whence they went by hoy to Whitstable, and across the channel.

Jimmy Wather and Thomas Scraggs of Whitstable were reported to be deep in the business."

For those who know the propensity of old Whitstable people to fit a nickname to everyone, this last sentence provides a valuable clue that it must have been Feaste who gave Jones the information for his report, as only Whitstable people would know to whom the names applied. Moreover, it was obvious that Feaste cleverly revealed no more than was obvious to the Authorities, namely that part of the traffic which dealt with the monied or superiour classes. The general escape route through Convicts Wood was never revealed even if it was known to those in authority.

Certainly Thomas Goodwin a highly respected farmer, Churchwarden and Overseer of the Poor was committing no crime by galloping through the main street of the town or riding slowly along a lonely country lane, stopping now and again to view the surrounding landscape. Writing his memories about 1850 an old man named Putwain recorded these words. "There was a carrier or receiver on shore named Tom Goodwin who would run his horse through the streets at a fearful speed and no one ever dare touch that horse, for he would certainly be knocked down. My Grandfather said that it would be the death of him."

What happened to Feaste at Bow Street in January 1812 we can only surmise, but some light is thrown on the subject by the writings of Louis Vanhille, a famous escaper, who had been Purser of the Pandour Privateer. He escaped from Dartmoor on August 21st 1812, and after moving about for some time he left Abergavenny on September 21st 1812 and made his way to Falmouth, where he met Thomas Feaste Moore alias Captain Thomas Harman at the Blue Anchor Inn. These particulars were copied by M. Pariset who claimed that at that time Harman was in the Government service having been pardoned for his misdeeds as an escape agent on condition that he made use of his experience by giving the Government information about intending escapers. Referring to this Francis Abell said that he could not find that Moore was ever thus employed.

Be that as it may, it is next to impossible to sift the wheat from the chaff where Feaste is concerned, but we do have an authentic picture of him again the next year.

In July 1813 a stranger was seen in Kelso, Scotland furtively carrying a trunk to the Cross Keys Inn, from which he presently went in a post-chaise to Lauder. He was not recognised, but frequent escapes from the town had awakened the vigilance of the Agent, and the suspicious behaviour of this stranger at the inn determined that official to pursue and arrest him. The trunk was found to belong to Dagues, a French Officer, and contained the clothes of three other officers on parole, and from the fact that the stranger had made inquiries about a coach for Edinburgh, it was clear that an arrangement was nipped in the bud. It appeared fairly certain that the officers were to follow, pick up the trunk at Edinburgh and get on a boat at Leith.

Feaste was disguised, but the next morning the agent from Kelso saw at once that he answered to the description of a man which had been circulated throughout the kingdom, and he sent him to Jedburgh Jail in safe custody while he communicated with London.

London just did not want to know and were certainly not grateful to the over zealous official. In the end it was left to no less a person than the Solicitor General to decide the best course to take. He gave it as his opinion that it was better that Feaste should be detained as a deserter from the Navy rather than as an aider of escaping prisoners, on the ground that there were no sufficiently overt acts on the part of the French prisoners to show an intention to escape. Only very patient and long research through many records could reveal what really happened to Feaste. He later claimed that in 1813 he was entered into his Majesty's Dockyard at Woolwich. These were his own words and could mean that he was employed on convict labour there. Furthermore, he says, that in 1815 he, with thirteen others, was sent to his Majesty's Dockyard in Gibraltar. His wife apparently died in 1817. However, we have no proof that Feaste ever returned to Whitstable after the war ended in 1815. Nevertheless, there are indications that he was the James Moore who was living in dire poverty at No. 2 Hope Street, Hackney Road, Middlesex in 1839.

Feaste's vessels continued to be maintained and used at Whitstable, their subsequent history is of interest. The Two Sisters was re-registered at Whitstable on October 31st 1842. The Whitstable was re-registered by William Edenden on September 12th 1825 and sold to William Andrews on July 1st 1839. These names are of interest in view of the fact that William Edenden was a witness at Feaste's marriage and that Mrs Feaste's maiden name was Andrews. The Elizabeth was sold to

Richard Harris	August 29th 1825
Edward Laraman	April 13th 1847
William Olive	October 9th 1847
Broken up	1850

During those few eventful years before peace came in 1815, thanks to the demands of the war, the number of vessels which could be released to combat the smuggling was very restricted. Nevertheless, they presented an additional hazard to be avoided by those vessels which had escaped prisoners on board.

During the period in question, the Whitstable men were on the whole able to carry on their trade without being caught. The local newspapers do, however, contain a few references to some of the government cutters such as the Griffin, Sea Gull, Lively, Otter, Tiger and Swallow. These vessels were stationed at different places with instructions to patrol certain coastlines. Particulars regarding the Success will serve to illustrate the general procedure.

She was a Cutter stationed to patrol from the Spile Buoy to the Nore, and her complement was:

1800 Commander William Broadbank £ 50 per annum
Mate Richard Broadbank £ 35 per annum
15 mariners at £ 18. 5. 0. each per annum
Victualling 1/- per diem

1805 Commander Thomas Gibbs £ 50 per annum
Mate Richard Broadbank £ 35 per annum
15 mariners at £ 18. 5. 0. each per annum
Victualling 1/5 per diem

1810 Commander Alexander Greet £100 per annum
Mate Richard Broadbank £ 60 per annum
Deputed Mariner at £1. 5. 0. per month
15 mariners at £ 2. 0. 0. each per month
Victualling, Commander and Mate at 3/- each per diem
15 Mariners at 1/6 each per diem

Fire and Candles 1/6 each per month.

In these days of rapid change it is a privilege to have spoken with men whose grandfathers have told them how they met and talked with the French prisoners of war and the convicts as they passed through Whitstable, and how after peace came in 1815 they talked with gangs of mowers who had stood in the squares at Waterloo with their comrades musket barrels resting on their shoulders, the muskets being fired until they were red hot and their faces became permanently scorched.

26

Could those prisoners visit once again the scenes of their earthly torment there are still a few things they would recognise, the Old Red House at Seasalter,[3] the little chancel of the Old Church,[9] the high protective banks of Church Lane.

Can it be that, despite its change of name, strange shadowy figures are still to be seen furtively climbing Cut Throat Lane[10] and admiring the glorious view from the top,[11] or that the ghostly outline of a lone horseman may be observed on dark nights silently moving along the lonely Pye Alley Lane with pitiful rags of shapeless humanity moving from bush to bush or rising from the roadside ditch. Is there no one living who has seen mysterious lights moving about the deserted Pye Alley Farm House[14] or shining from the little window?[16] The little Bogs Hole Brook[18] still gurgles its twisting way through green meadows and the ghostly shades of Convicts Wood to the ancient oak near the road at the Red Bridge[21] where spiritual hands stretch out for the food left by the kind souls, and the point of Swalecliffe Rock[25] is a place to avoid on a dark, cold, windy, night.

27